Too good to be true?

Well, it is true and there is no lies in my personal experience in money making over the Internet.

I am not a professional writer, I just write because it helps me fresh my mind and it is healthy with my brain and best of all it is profitable hobby.

And I am not a native English speaker but that is not an excuse of not earning money online.

Follow me and you will not regret.

Remember, you will only need your free time to earn over $12,000 so if you are lazy or not willing to work hard in your part for free then there's nothing will happened with your dreams.

I will include my life story before I will tell you how to make $12,000 using just one website.

Don't feel bored with me because it is worth reading and most especially you will surely earn money for free. You need to be patient and let's start it here!

If you cannot finish reading my introduction, then you will find it hard or not be able to really make more money using the Internet because patient and willingness is your key to success.

I would like to share a bit about myself. You can call me Charlotte or Lot for short.

I am single and I am looking for my life time partner someday or now, who knows!

I am an orphan and I was raised with an old woman who happened to be my grandmother.

She passed away several years ago and from that time on, I was living alone in our small barn atop of the hills. This was my picture taken inside the barn using a self-timer camera that I borrowed from my classmate.

Check more about me here "My Personal Life Story".

After my grandmother died I lived in this barn alone, I raised goats and chickens, planted vegetables and corns for my food supply.

Few years passed, the typhoon hits my barn and destroyed my only one shelter. This was the picture of my destroyed barn.

This was my bed that was made of bamboo before the typhoon damaged the barn. As you can see in the picture besides the bed was a plastic and I used it to cover my stuff or myself when the rain came because it got wet the whole barn including me too (wink).

Below was the picture of an anthill underneath my bed.

This was the anthill built up from the ground up to the bamboo floor and then almost touch to my bamboo bed. Look at the picture below.

Sometimes the ants crawled in my head or hair because when I fall asleep my long hair touched the floor.

This picture showed the natural spring or water from the ground where I fetched water for my daily consumption. I had to walk for about 30 minutes one way and additional 30 minutes back just to get water for my drink.

And then I graduated from High School with less than 40 students at that time. I already living alone and my grandmother had already passed away.

After my high school graduation, I applied for Government Scholarship and luckily I passed with the test and enrolled in freshmen college in Cebu City. This was my first uniform and first time in the city.

I was boarding in the city and I slept in the bed frame with the hole in it. I could not barely stretch my legs because the room was really small. And it was beneath the riverbank and I can smell the bad odor from the stagnant water and also dead rats floating right in the back of this holed bed. At one time, a muddy kitty crawled in my head while I was asleep. The housemaid of my landlady was my witness.

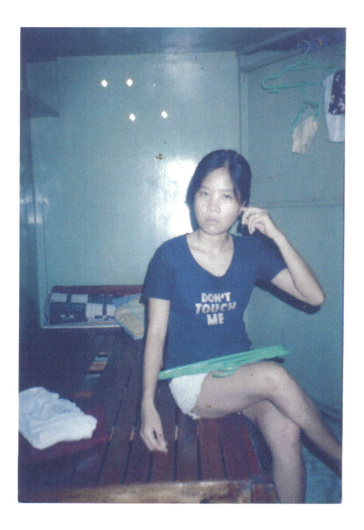

I rented in a small room boarding house where drugs and addicts were rampant in the area and also drunkards standbys. But it was the only place where cheap shelter was available for me at that time. The wall has holes and also the bed and my blanket was also holed blanket and old he he.

When I was in the city, I was able to mingle with rich students and went to their home with swimming pool. I also met rich girls who had used clothes for me and then later that year, I learned how to use computer because in my public high school there was no typewriter nor computer.

I also learned and developed to dressed up myself as attractive and sexy in the public. I was not used to wear sexy clothes but I was kind of learning how the city life looks like.

I lived with 5 girls or students in my new boarding house and they loved using the Internet. I was alone most of the times so they encouraged me to go with them and use the computer and then while I was waiting for them to finish their projects, the computer attendant taught me on how to create my first email which was Yahoo and then she told me to start chatting and look for the chat room so that I won't be bored while waiting for my board mates.

So I chatted different guys and one of them was really interested to see me in person and I was really surprised and I did not mention anything to my friends because I was shy to let them know, they will just laugh at me if I did.

Few more tries, I was addicted in chatting and I was able to create a profile in a dating website online. When I was bored, I just went to the Internet Cafe and stayed there until I felt sleepy.

From that time on, I met an American guy who was willing to meet me as soon as he can.

To make the story short, I came here in United States with a fiancee visa but when I arrived my fiance did not tell me that he was living with another woman. So I run away from him and now I am still single.

And I stayed with a friend and I was looking for an income, I have no car nor driver's license at that time and luckily I found this one website that is making me money every month until now. I made about more than $12,000 and I am new, and if I will keep writing and searching for more passive income online then I will make more for extra earnings for free.

I included my story so that you will know what it will take to really earn money for free and make even more if you are motivated enough to succeed. Giving you the steps are not enough if you have no motivation in doing it or inspiration to start with, so my story will give you a lesson that if I did it then why can't you?

If you are motivated enough with my personal story then you will earn more money than I do in this website. I will include my earnings screen, this is my real income and this is not edited just to look like impressive.

This is my real earnings of $12,000. I spent less time after I made my first $6,726.15 but if you work hard then you will earn money as a full time income if you really want it bad.

The picture is not really a good shot but it is clear enough to see the figures in it. I will post different shots but the same screen to make you see it clearly.

<< Previous Year | Next Year

Total Earnings	Payment Status	Payment Issued
$187.26 USD	Completed from Received	$359.95 USD
$359.95 USD	Carryover	$0.00 USD
$525.59 USD	Completed from Received	$525.59 USD
$676.41 USD	Completed from Received	$676.41 USD
$668.46 USD	Completed from Received	$668.46 USD
$791.91 USD	Completed from Received	$791.91 USD
$908.08 USD	Completed from Received	$908.08 USD
$868.23 USD	Completed from Received	$868.23 USD
$866.19 USD	Completed from Received	$866.19 USD
$874.07 USD	Completed from Received	$874.07 USD
$6,726.15 USD	--	$6,538.89 USD

<< Previous Year |

This is another screen shot with the date in it. This is my real earnings and I never spend a dime to earn this just my free time in just one website.

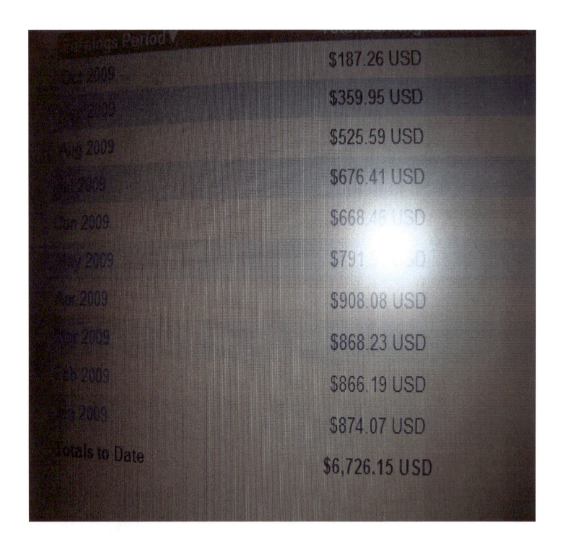

I find it hard to speak fluent in English so this is just what I have. And if you are an English native then you will earn more than I do.

This is another screen shot.

	Payment Status	Payment Issued
SD	Completed from Received	$775.19 USD
SD	Completed from Received	$863.01 USD
SD	Completed from Received	$756.30 USD
SO	Completed from Received	$635.42 USD
SD	Completed from Received	$482.73 USD
SD	Completed from Received	$511.33 USD
SD	Completed from Received	$439.85 USD
SD	Completed from Received	$531.67 USD
SD	Completed from Received	$448.14 USD
SD	Completed from Received	$420.70 USD
SD	Completed from Received	$125.96 USD
SD	Completed from Received	$70.60 USD
USD	--	$6,060.90 USD

By just looking at this real screen shots won't get you anywhere, so you will need to do the work first and then compare your screen shots to mine later. The picture is not good and I just took a screen shot with my camera and then adjust the size but this should be enough reference if you are willing to earn for real.

So here's to start the free challenge in online money making.

==The steps to follow on how I made my first $12,000 for free online and just for one website $$==

1. You will need to get an email address.
   You can use yahoo or gmail account and these are free or any valid email that you can get.

2. Create your PayPal account for free. Visit www.paypal.com.
   This is totally free to have one and this is the only way that you can get paid for now with this website that I am earning money from for free. You will get monthly deposit to your PayPal account.

3. Prepare your credit cards or bank account. These are not very important but you can use this to add in your Paypal account and then become a verified Paypal user.

4. You need to be in the United States or have a valid U.S resident address and also your PayPal address should match with your billing address or resident.

5. You also need to be able to produce a valid Social Security Number which is issued in the United States.

6. Of course, you need to have a real name to fill up properly with the money making program in order to get paid. Do not steal someone's identity just to get your paycheck.

7. It would also be helpful if you can speak good English but if you can write simple instructions in English language then that will do it.
   It is important to follow the simple rules and agreement set forth in every website or in this website.

   Don't ignore the rules.

Alright, let's start the steps to start making money online.

I will add in the end if I missed something. Note: This book is published in an eBook form and a hard copy one, so the link will not work if you are buying the printed form but if you are buying the electronic form then you will be able to follow the link included in this book.

1. You have to read my own Profile in the website that I am talking about. But if you found this information through the hard copy of my book, then just visit the website called "eHow" or go to their website at www.eHow.com.

And create your new account for free. You will not be required with your financial information except for PayPal email address and then fill up the form to sign up with their compensation program. You will not receive your income without your PayPal account. So it is important to sign up with your PayPal.

You can also become an author or as an expert in this website and earn even more money from writing that way. Browse around in the site or ask other users or members by visiting their community forum because everything that you want to know is there waiting for you.

2. Don't be too rush to start everything without reading all the steps and all the tips here or you can go on and manage yourself to start earning money and hopefully you will not come back here and complained why you did not make enough money to buy a needle to poke your eyes (joke) and don't do it because it hurts (common sense please)!

Sometimes you don't really need the step by step to start earning money online but a real proof that this program will work to anyone, who knows how to write and learn the laws of course. Always put yourself in somebody's shoes as long as it doesn't stink yourself. Everything has rules to follow so abide them all to avoid getting into trouble.

3. Knowing where to go is not enough if you are not equipped with the knowledge and motivation to reach your goal or follow the direction. You will need a real experience from a person like me or anyone to motivate your brain to start earning. So if you are ready then follow me on my own personal Blog.

Or visit: http://myehowearnings.blogspot.com/2009/02/how-i-saved-my-ehow-earnings.html

4. When you are ready with the challenge in online money making, do not forget to double check your PayPal email address because this is the only way for now to get your paycheck every month and if you give them the wrong one then you will have to keep waiting for nothing.

5. Do not forget to visit the forum in the website because that's where all the members are chatting or talking about the issues or helpful tips for everybody and most of all enjoy meeting new friends virtually.

These are the additional tips for you to see: For eBook readers.

Monthly Earnings Schedule
Earn Money this way too
I Stopped Writing but Earning

OK!

If for any reasons you are not making money from the tips you are reading, then do not hesitate to contact me "Here" and leave questions or messages that you want me to answer and I will make it sure that you will earn money just like me provided that you tried all the tips I listed or give you.

Remember that I am not writing the whole day to earn the $12,000 but I only write once in a while and honestly I stopped writing already for the new goal in life. You can read everything in my Personal Blog.

Good luck!

I would like to leave this page blank for you to write your own personal story in making money using this one website. Tell us or share it with me how your experience went in this "Website".

Your blank space start here:

Write your story this
space---

Here you can post your earning screen shots:

List your own tips and feedback that will help others to make money online:

Anything you want to say negative or positive as long as it is helpful in money making:

I will also update my very latest look in 2009. This is my new look now and I grow up a bit (smile).

After saving all my online earnings, I was able to buy these following:

This is an empty land and I bought this in the Philippines for very cheap because the owner was in a hospital so the sale was desperate.

This was the vacant lot in the above picture and now it has corns and other vegetables. My new found relatives planted the different root crops and they also built their own house in the land. They were not closed to me before when I was there but recently my relatives started to show some love for me, I didn't really make it into a negative conclusion because everyone makes mistakes one way or another. So they are now the one who tilled this land and make their living through planting different root crops.

I also bought this coconut farm for a very cheap price as well.

The land has also corns and bananas. I have my long distant relatives tilled the land and harvest the corns for their own consumption. I just recently become closer to them but I grew up without them. It's a very long story to include the story about them but I will probably tell in the future.

And now!

Welcome to my new built barn! This is another thing that I spend with my online earnings.

Just me here... So...

Find your own way to work stress-free and enjoy whatever you do in your life everyday, that's the secret in real happiness. "Money is just a choice to make yourself happy sometimes, but it is not needed in order to live" that's my personal view.

In conclusion, I felt so rich now even if I just have few dollars in my wallet. The difference is that, the Dollar Currency has more value compared to the Philippine Peso. So if I saved from my online earnings for about $12,000 then multiply that to our currency exchange right now for about P45 (Pesos) the result is about half million pesos (540,000 Pesos) which is a lot of money if you have no family to feed and in my case I am an "Orphan".

I have no parents and I just recently become closer to my long distant relatives and still manage to save and buy something that I never had before. I felt really lucky to be in the United States even if my relationship was not working as I hoped when I left from my country.

Most of all, I am thankful that a one website can make me money that can supplement my expenses and still live the life that I have missed for a long time since I was a kid.

Recently, I stopped writing on that website because I met someone whom I think I am in love with but I am hesitant to trust anyone because of what had happened to me in the beginning but I will set aside my past and learned to move on and give someone a try and see if it will work someday!

I thought I was going to get married but I guess it is a big challenge to find some one who really cares for what I am, not for what I can give physically or mentally.

I am looking for real love so tell your friends that I am still available and he can find me here (smile).

Have a wonderful day to everyone and good luck for whatever you do in life!

At the end...

Things can go wrong sometimes but remember that the only way to fail is to surrender. So keep trying no matter what. Good luck!

Sometimes, life is like sailing in a fishing boat in the middle of the ocean and we do not know when the storm strikes us all. So be prepared even if you think that it will never happen to you ever, because we just don't know what to expect in the future.

On the final note check these words out:

1. Google Adsense--this is where all the money come from either you have your own website or just contributing to someone's website. Learn about their Adwords program because you can use it to guide you the right key words that have more value than others. You can also advertise your own business if you have one or just educate yourself to equip your mind with the latest trends in today's technology.

2. Writer's Compensation Program--- if you want to just contribute to others website instead of making or building your own website then you will need to know what is the term compensation is all about. You will have to sign up with this compensation program in order to get paid with your work as a freelance writer.

3. Article Marketing---this is where you will advertise your articles through writing. If you have an article about how to make money then write about it again and submit it through article directories or search engine. You can submit your articles or website on Yahoo or Google for free. Do not submit it often because that is called spamming and you will be out in no time.

4. Networking--- you also need how to socialize because in today's trends this kind of advertisement is really effective. It seems that everybody needs a buddy in today's economy so start looking for social bookmarking sites like My Space, Face Book, You Tube, Live Journal, Blogger, e How, Hub Pages, and many more.

5. Writing---sometimes we think that everything is too easy most especially if we heard the word everyday but there are rules and agreements to follow to make the writing more successful in the long run. So it is important to know on how to write a simple article that is not in violation of anyone's copy rights. Learn about the word plagiarism and infringement, trademark and publisher or author.

6. Taxes---don't forget to file your taxes in your online earnings because the website will forward your self-employment tax form to the IRS and if you will not report your earnings then you will get audited or get screwed at the end. It might take time but why wait for the trouble? Just do it and...

Have fun!

www.ingramcontent.com/pod-product-compliance
Lightning Source LLC
Chambersburg PA
CBHW041428050326
40689CB00003B/706